Successful Interviewing

Successful Interviewing

A Talent-Focused Approach to Successful Recruitment and Selection

Dr. Tony Miller

BEP BUSINESS EXPERT PRESS

First published in 2017 by
Business Expert Press, LLC
222 East 46th Street, New York, NY 10017
www.businessexpertpress.com

ISBN-13: 978-1-63157-833-5 (paperback)
ISBN-13: 978-1-63157-834-2 (e-book)

Business Expert Press Human Resource Management and Organizational Behavior Collection

Collection ISSN: 1946-5637 (print)
Collection ISSN: 1946-5645 (electronic)

Cover and interior design by S4Carlisle Publishing Services Private Ltd., Chennai, India

First edition: 2017

10 9 8 7 6 5 4 3 2 1

Printed in the United States of America.

*Dedicated to all Recruitment professionals worldwide
who really want to make a difference.*

Abstract

This practical guide to recruiting talented people incorporates the latest innovations in interviewing techniques. The very latest research shows that a process approach to interviewing provides greater structure and has the potential for significantly reducing bias. Learn how to deter and filter the poor performers and benefit from structured prewritten score able questions that will really make a difference to interviewing effectiveness.

In a time where all organizations are striving to get the best talented people, it makes sense for organizations to upgrade and review their interviewing procedures and incorporate whatever techniques are available to reduce interviewing errors. The evidence shows that many HR functions have failed in the past to understand the long-term financial consequences of poor performance or to realize that talented people do so much more work than other employees. Financial examples are shown in this book using data from the 2015 work done survey.

Successful talent recruitment is a key management tool and is critical to any organization's long-term success. This book gives you a detailed guide to the entire nine-step process with clear worked examples.

Keywords

Business success, competence, interview, interviewing, performance, productivity, recruitment, selection, talent, testing.

Contents

Author's Foreword

The recruitment and selection process is the gateway to any organization. It is interesting that most of the world's highest financial performing companies have rigorous recruitment processes and recruitment is seen as a key business objective. These companies unfortunately are in the minority.

The goal of a well-planned selection method is to pick the person who will best fit in the job position in terms of abilities and skills, but also the one who will be able to offer value to the team and the organization. A bad choice of employees can cause great damages to an organization, and depending on their position in it, this can vary from intoxicating the organization's culture to costing it large amounts of money.

I have been running master classes on recruitment for over two decades in almost every sector and all over the world; it is sad to reflect that most attendees still have a very naive approach to the very serious business of recruitment. One of the most widely observed phenomena is the fact that often, personality aspects of the candidates are overlooked. In many corporations, especially in those that are of high technical nature, the tasks and questions in the interviews are highly based on technical aspects and therefore personality aspects are ignored. In this book, the use of personality profiling and its essentiality for the selection process will be discussed.

Recent evidence shows that repeatedly organizations are tricked and deceived by applicants—sometimes the results have had dire consequences. The chapters of this book emphasize on the importance of the training of interviewers so that they can be able to detect impression-management and faking.

This book offers a process approach that can be adopted by any organization for its recruitment. It is designed to eliminate bias as much as is possible and to bring rigor and organizational control on this critical process.

The concise book offers help for professional recruiters and anyone in the organization who has responsibility for improving organizational performance through recruiting or promoting talented people.

Acknowledgments

I wish to thank all the participants of my recruitment master classes over the last 3 years who convinced me that this book was needed. Also, the 2015 survey of over 1100 managers who provided details of hours worked in the three critical bands and the fact that poor performers were recruited by someone and as a consequence have cost their organizations massive sums in lost productivity.

Rather than use old research to establish certain recruitment factors, this books incorporates the work of two dedicated research professionals

Luke Treglown, Sr. Research Assistant, and Kelly Petropoulou, University College London whose brief was to research only the latest proven work relating to the nine stages of successful recruitment.

Why a Process?

If you were to ask 10 of your managers "what's the best way to interview," I suspect you would get 10 different answers, each convinced that their way was the best. A look through LinkedIn shows what a vast range of different ideas there are on what should be done, ranging from the quest to make recruitment as cheap as possible to outlandish ideas that defy belief.

Every time you recruit, you have the opportunity to make a decision—either good or bad. You can recruit talented people, average people, or people who are and are likely always to be poor performers. The financial crunch between 2012 and 2014 has shown all of us that most organizations were overstaffed, and reductions in organizational numbers in many cases resulted in higher productivity and greater organizational efficiency. The reason that numbers could and have been reduced is that those companies had a disproportionate amount of poor and average performers—and yes, someone had recruited them.

A survey completed in 2013 in the Middle East of over 1,000 employees in 110 large companies showed that talented people do almost six times more work than poor performers; the financial implications of inadequate recruitment are massive.

The traditional face-to-face interview

The reasons that just face-to-face recruitment fails are a combination of the following. This is not an opinion but is based on reliable current studies and fact.

- **Validity**
  The unreliability of the face-to-face interview due to bias and the fact that they do not measure what they are designed to do.
- **Interviewer motivation**
  Because interviews are a long process, attention spans wane. Accuracy of the interview is based on the interviewer's ability to pick the right applicant. If testing is omitted, this becomes an unreliable method.

- **Office politics**

  Office politics can result in a significant blow to interview validity. Interviews to be relatively easy to "fix" due to interviewers favoring certain candidates; they can nod and smile to encourage those they like, while provoking unfavorable applicants with negative or blunt remarks. This can mean that the interview acts as a stage for office politics and power networking, with members of the interview board lobbying inferior candidates because they match their interests (Bozionelos, 2005). Woodzicka and LaFrance (2005) also demonstrated that interviewers who ask mildly sexually harassing questions to female interviewees cause dramatic drops in interview performance; the candidates spoke less fluently, gave lower-quality answers, and asked less job-related questions.

- **Lack of training**

  The vast majority of people who interview have been inadequately trained, or not trained at all. The results are apparent as interviewers do not tell candidates what dimensions will be covered/assessed in the interviews, as this will cause applicants to prepare answers that say the right thing/what interviewers want to hear. Klehe et al. (2008) found that transparency greatly increased the construct-validity of the interview dimensions; when applicants were able to prepare, their answers better reflected what the questions were actually asking. Furthermore, the increase in content validity meant that the strengths and weaknesses between applicants were more easily distinguishable, as answers were no longer incomparable due to the vague/invalid nature of interview questions.

- **Unstructured interviews**

  An unstructured interview with potential future employees is a method used by managers in order to "read between the lines," size them up, and ascertain whether or not they are the right person for the position. Managers have a heavy preference for unstructured interviews because it allows them to go with their gut and use their intuition, potentially spotting idiosyncrasies that would be missed in analytical measures. Managers commonly overestimate the influence of intuition, while dramatically underestimating the validity of more robust measures (i.e., paper-and-pencil tests, structured interviews, etc.), in "X-factor"/"right stuff" thinking for finding talented employees.

- ○ Myers (2002) "interview illusion"—an unstructured, intuition-based interview may focus more on a candidate's declared intentions and future behavior, but these are likely to be a less useful predictor than their past performance.
- ○ Lievens, Highhouse, and De Corte (2005)—managers placed more emphasis on competencies assessed by unstructured interviews than competencies measured by tests, irrespective of what the competency was.
- ○ Managers emphasized the importance of extroversion over general mental ability when the former was ascertained through unstructured interview while the latter was found through pencil-and-paper test. Yet, managers preferred general mental ability when found through unstructured interview than Extroversion when decided by tests. Therefore, this is evidence that managers rely heavily on their instincts when sizing up an individual.

The panel interview

One of the most potentially ineffective ways of interviewing, yet many organizations are still using it. The reason they do is to avoid accountability, to be seen to be involved, and in some instances people are on the panel so they can show their peers how clever they are.

Candidates often find the panel interview overwhelming and intimidating and for that reason introverts do not perform well in such conditions. The most effective would be two people interviewing, the line manager together with the interviewing professional. Secondary interviews should also be avoided, as this is normally a sign that no one wants accountability for the final decision-making.

The process approach

A process approach helps to avoid most of our problem areas and also the underlying issue that managers, in the main, only recruit people they like. That "like" is often made up of the most amazing preconceived ideas that would not survive any sort of rational audit. The process approach is a way of having a standardized format across the organization and ensuring a conformance to standards.

The process approach may need to be modified to fit individual organizational needs and that is your choice.

The process consists of nine sequential steps—each very important to the total objective of recruiting great people.

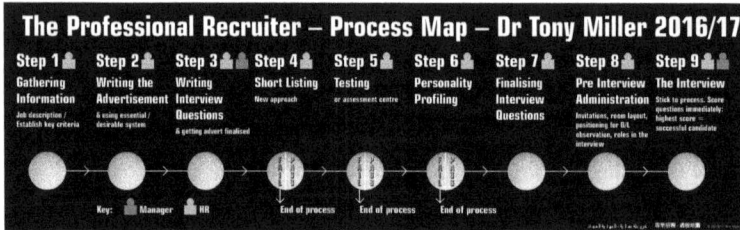

The Professional Recruiter – Process Map – Dr Tony Miller 2016/17

References

Bozionelos, N. (2005). When the inferior candidate is offered the job: The selection interview as a political and power game. Human Relations, 58(12), 1605–1631.

Brtek, M.D., & Motowildo, S.J. (2002). Effects of procedure and outcome accountability on interview validity. Journal of Applied Psychology, 87, 185–191.

Budnick, C.J., Kowal, M., & Santuzzi, A.M. (2015). Social anxiety and the ironic effects of positive interviewer feedback. Anxiety, Stress, and Coping, 28(1), 71–87. doi: 10.1080/10615806.2014.919386.

Klehe, U.T., König, C.J., Richter, G.M., Kleinmann, M., & Melchers, K.G. (2008). When the inferior candidate is offered the job: The selection interview as a political and power game. Human Performance, 21, 107–137.

Lievens, F., Highhouse, S., & De Corte, W. (2005). The importance of traits and abilities in supervisors' hirability decisions as a function of method of assessment. Journal of Occupational and Organisational Psychology, 78, 453–470.

McCarthy, J., & Goffin, R. (2004). Measuring job interview anxiety: Beyond weak knees and sweaty palms. Personnel Psychology, 57, 607–637.

Myers, D. (2002). Intuition: Its Powers and Perils. New Haven: Yale University Press.

Woodzicka, J.A., & LaFrance, M. (2005). The effect of sexual harassment on women's performance in a job interview. Sex Roles, 53(1–2), 67–77.

Swart T. (2014). The Neuroscience of Bias. CIPD People Management.

STEP 1

Gathering Information

Always the first question is "Do we need to fill this post?" Organizations become slaves of habit and therefore omit challenging every newly vacant post. Especially in larger organizations, it is always useful to check out future needs using workforce planning (Miller, 2013). Some posts may no longer be needed by the organization; therefore, keeping them active for the sake of tradition is unnecessary and costly.

If the answer to the above is yes, then does the position need a full-time employee? How is technology impacting that job and its role within your organization?

Once the green light is on to recruit, check out the job description and establish if it's really up-to-date. This part of the recruitment process is supposed to be done each year by the line manager or whenever performance appraisal is carried out.

Job descriptions seem to vary vastly, from just the briefest of outlines to detailed documents, which specify how performance is to be measured.

Whichever you have, one thing is critical either now or at stage two—you must find out the key criteria for the job. This criterion is the essence of what's critical for the person to have or display when they are in the post. It is ultimately the line manager's responsibility to provide this information and keep it updated.

Depending on where you are in the world, this goes by different names:

- Key criteria
- Critical behavioral qualities
- Deal breakers
- Key competencies (Rowe 1995).

If you have bio-data profiles of the job, you would at this stage check that the data are up-to-date.

Armed with sound information, you are ready for Step 2.

Reference

Rowe, C. (1995). Clarifying the use of competence and competency models in recruitment, assessment and staff development. Industrial and Commercial Training, 27(11), 12–17.

Miller, T. (2013). New Workforce Planning: From A to Z. Chelmsford: Management Performance Solutions Ltd.

STEP 2

Writing the Advertisement

Ask any fisherman about how to catch the specific type of fish you want, and they will reply—it depends on the bait you use. The same is true about attracting candidates: it's all about writing the advertisement. Regardless of where the advertisement is placed or which media is used, the construction of a good advertisement is essential if we are trying to attract the best people for our organization.

In this example, we look at an advertisement for a Senior Finance Manager who will be running a finance department of 30 people.

The advertisement can be broken down into four parts.

Part One: PR

The advertisement gives us the first opportunity of showing what a great organization we are—use the advertisement not only to attract the right candidates, but also as a PR tool for your organization. Please remember this, as the whole of the recruitment process is about creating and demonstrating a positive aspect of your organization. You want good applicants to be attracted to your organization and to apply—the advertisement is your shop window (Lievens @ De Paepe, 2004).

> One of the fastest growing and successful pharmaceutical companies in Switzerland, employing more than 3,500 people, has a rare vacancy for an Sr. Finance Manager based in our headquarters in Geneva. Salary in excess of €189,000.00 with an impressive range of benefits and a target-linked bonus scheme.

Part Two: Job Outline

Outline of the job. This should be a broad-brush explication of the main duties involved and can normally be taken from the job description. In this section, it's very important that you use the words that will attract the right personality type for the job advertised. Broadly speaking, introverts are attracted to jobs in finance, audit, research, IT, some legal jobs, backroom jobs in trading shares, archives, etc. They are normally motivated by words such as attention to detail, strict adherence to rules and deadlines, working to tight fiscal limits, tight regulatory control. Extroverts would be more motivated by power words such as highly competitive environment, challenging work, high risk, opportunity to excel and prove yourself, large amount of social interaction. Extroverts are normally found in sales, marketing, PR, advertising, TV, and radio.

For this job and the context of the work, our power words would come from those of an introvert disposition.

This key position involves managing the day-to-day running of a busy finance department of 30 employees delivering financial service to our business. Delivery to tight deadlines and meticulous attention to detail are essential. As a company listed on the Swiss Exchange, we need our Senior Financial Manager to lead and drive our team in terms of International Financial Reporting Standards and their development. Our Senior Financial Manager will also need significant expertise in Swiss taxation legislation.

Part Three: Requirements

This is where we list the key criteria, which should be available in the job description. As mentioned before, this is sometimes referred to as the key competencies, or deal breakers. We list these in two columns—Essentials and Desirables. This makes it easy for prospective candidates to clearly see what's needed and at a later stage make the job of writing interview questions easier and more precise (Brtek, and Motowildo, 2002). It also gives us a template to do very precise short-listing.

This part of the selection process is very important as it sets the basis for the Psychological Contract between the organization and its potential employee. It is the first and basic idea that the candidate gets of what will be expected of them throughout their stay in the organization.

Essentials	Desirables
• Chartered or Certified Accountants or CPAs only need apply	• MBA from *Times*-published top 20 universities
• Min of 9 years' experience in a similar industry	• French speaking and writing
• English, Swiss/German written and spoken	• Current European driving license
• Management of a similar-size function	
• Use of any major database-driven accounting software system, such as Oracle, SAP, SAGE, Sun, or similar	
• Full understanding of Swiss government financial regulations and IFRS	
• Management of organization's budget cycle	
• Can demonstrate successful matrix management	
• Managing teams	

Part Four: Information

You need to state any other information that the candidate needs to be aware of—where to get more information. Closing date and the power sentence that will stop time wasters, the unqualified, and other unsuitable people from applying.

Details of this position showing the organizational chart, department structure, full range of benefits, and either an online application or downloadable copy are available on our website link www.swisspharma/Deparmtnet_finance_manager.org.

Closing date for all applications is 26/02/2015.

A current (no more than 6 months old) head-and-shoulders passport-type photo must be attached to your application.

PLEASE NOTE, all successful short-listed applicants will be tested.

At Step 2 of our recruitment process, we have now constructed our advertisement—to attract good people and, importantly, dissuade others from applying and wasting our time. The process of writing the advertisement is best done with the line manager as it is critical to get the Essentials and Desirables list right, as it will be used for the short-listing and for prewriting our interview questions at Step 3.

One of the fastest growing and successful pharmaceutical companies in Switzerland, employing more than 3,500 people, has a rare vacancy for a Sr. Finance Manager based in our headquarters in Geneva. Salary in excess of €189,000.00 with an impressive range of benefits and a target-linked bonus scheme.

This key position involves managing the day-to-day running of a busy finance department of 30 employees delivering financial service to our business. Delivery to tight deadlines and meticulous attention to detail are essential. As a company listed on the Swiss Exchange, we need our Senior Financial Manager to lead and drive our team in terms of International Financial Reporting Standards and their development. Our Senior Financial Manager will also need significant expertise in Swiss taxation legislation.

Essentials	Desirables
• Chartered or Certified Accountants or CPAs only need apply	• MBA from *Times*-published top 20 universities
• Min of 9 years' experience in a similar industry	• French speaking and writing
• Managing teams	• Current European driving license
• English, Swiss/German written and spoken	
• Management of a similar-size function	
• Use of any major database-driven accounting software system, such as Oracle, SAP, SAGE, Sun, or similar	
• Full understanding of Swiss government financial regulations and IFRS	
• Management of organization's budget cycle	
• Can demonstrate successful matrix management	

Details of this position showing the organizational chart, department structure, full range of benefits, and either an online application or downloadable copy are available on our website link www.swisspharma/Deparmtnet_finance_manager.org.

Closing date for all applications is 26/02/2015.

A current (no more than 6 months old) head-and-shoulders passport-type photo must be attached to your application.

PLEASE NOTE, all successful short-listed applicants will be tested.

Take care with the information you send the applicant. If you have a complete no-smoking policy, it needs to be mentioned. Even things like dress code should be included—all this information must be provided before the application is processed. We live in a world of increasing litigation, so ignore this small point at your peril.

Step 2: Summary

- The advertisement is a superb publicity tool—use it wisely.
- The advertisement must focus on the key criteria needed for the position to be successfully filled.
- The advertisement needs to clearly list the essentials and desirables in the lists. This then makes it easy at stage four—short-listing.
- Mention in the advertisement that all successful short-listed candidates will be tested, which will act as an automatic barrier for any dishonest people who are thinking of applying for the job.
- The cost of the advertisement is insignificant. HR people get oversensitive about the cost of interviewing—the cost does not really matter. Recruiting is such a major long-term investment that cutting costs on this process makes no sense at all.

Reference

Lievens @ De Paepe, 2004. An empirical investigation of interviewer-related factors that discourage the use of high structure interviews. Journal of Organizational Behavior 25, 29–46.

Brtek, M.D., and Motowildo, S.J. (2002). Effects of procedure and outcome accountability on interview validity. Journal of Applied Psychology, 87, 185–191.

STEP 3

Prewriting the Interview Questions

This is a great opportunity to save time and do a really good job. Often interviewers make up questions during the interview or give roughly the same question but sometimes with more of an explanation. This is a sign of consistency. It is not fair to all the candidates and introduces bias in various ways.

All the interview questions should be based on your key criteria and taken from your list of Essentials and Desirables. Working with the line manager gives you both the opportunity to examine the topic and write good experience-based questions to explore what your candidate has actually done in their previous jobs. Past experience is a good indicator of how they will actually fit into the vacant position in your organization.

So to recap, each key criterion will be a topic heading, and you will write four to six questions on each topic. During the interview, each of the topic questions will be scored out of 10, depending on how satisfying and suitable for the organization the answer is.

First, you need to decide how you are going to check each item on our Essentials list and Desirables list from your advertisement. These are going to be split between testing (T), questions (Q), and visual examination (V).

At this stage, we are only interested in the topics that we will ask questions on—the topic we shall select as an example is "Managing Teams."

Essentials	Desirables
• MBA from *Times*-published top 20 universities V	• French speaking and writing T
• Managing teams Q	• Current
• Min of 9 years' experience in a similar industry Q	• European driving license V
• Swiss/German written and spoken T	
• Management of a similar-size function Q	
• Use of any major database-driven accounting software system, such as Oracle, SAP, SAGE, Sun, or similar Q	
• Full understanding of government financial regulations and IFRS Q	
• Management of organization's budget cycle Q	
• Can demonstrate successful matrix management Q	

Key Criteria—Managing Teams

Q1. Please explain the techniques you use to motivate your team(s) in your current job.

Q2. When a dispute has arisen in your team—what actions need to be taken to resolve it?

Q3. What methodology have you used when selecting a member of your staff to work in a matrix or other department project?

Q4. How have you rewarded high-performing teams in your previous jobs?

Once you have four to six questions on the topic (above), then you can work through the rest from your advertisement.

- Minimum of 9 years' experience in a similar industry Q
- Management of a similar-size function Q
- Use of any major database-driven accounting software system, such as Oracle, SAP, SAGE, Sun, or similar Q
- Full understanding of government financial regulations and IFRS Q

- Management of organization's budget cycle Q
- Can demonstrate successful matrix management Q

In the workplace, writing the advertisement and carrying out this stage normally takes less than an hour. By writing the questions together, you are able to refine them and make them very clear. Every candidate will get exactly the same questions, and each of those questions will be scored out of 10—at the end of the interview, the person with the highest score gets the job. In this way, you can make sure that necessary questions are not omitted and the system scoring decreases the likelihood of interviewers' biases to play a role in the final selection.

I am sure you must be thinking how we do this for people who have no experience—graduates or first-job entrants. We have prewritten questions specifically for such people and will explain that later in Appendix 1. Usually with graduates, interviews involve competency-based questions that can be answered by using examples from their academic lives.

Summary: Step 3

- This step is a massive time saver.
- You will be able to see from the criteria which criteria need questions to be asked.
- Your questions should be a blend of experience-based competency and behavioral aspects.
- Talking the questions through with the line manager will vastly enhance the quality of interview questions you will ask.
- Four to six questions for each criterion.

STEP 4

Short-Listing

This is the first chance we get to see the response from our work to date. If we have done a good job, we should not have many applicants, but those who have applied will be of excellent quality. Nevertheless, there is always a high possibility of having applicants who may overestimate their abilities or try to fake some of the Essential and Desirable skills. Therefore, it is crucial that applicants are required to attach proof documents (e.g., certificates, diplomas, etc.).

This is the first stage of the process where bias can happen. In a video on recruitment, the film showed how biased selection can be by making decisions like "I don't like this one's writing" or "disregard this one, it's written in colored pen". Nevertheless, one has to keep in mind that these are completely unscientific arguments and should therefore not play any role in the final selection.

Today's laws will get you into court very quickly if you don't have robust and bias-free procedures in place.

So who should do the selection? Well, it's very straightforward: We need all the CVs that have all the Essential requirements—then as many that have all or some of the Desirables. Then the decision is made. A competent person in Human Resources can carry out that work.

To make every effort to remove the possibility of bias, it is suggested that those who will be doing the interview should not be involved in this part of the process.

If you have the ability to do so, the CV form or/and the online template can be laid out so that all the Essentials and Desirables are clearly listed, thereby making the job of short-listing easier and less likely to make a mistake.

Essentials	Desirables
• Chartered or Certified Accountants or CPAs only need apply	• MBA from *Times*-published top 20 universities
• Minimum of 9 years' experience in a similar industry	• French speaking and writing
• Managing teams	• Current European driving license
• English, Swiss/German written and spoken	
• Management of a similar-size function	
• Use of any major database-driven accounting software system, such as Oracle, SAP, SAGE, Sun, or similar	
• Full understanding of Swiss government financial regulations and IFRS	
• Management of organization's budget cycle	
• Can demonstrate successful matrix management	

Once the short-listing has been completed, inform those who are unsuccessful, and then make arrangements for testing and personality profiling or an assessment center to take place.

If we look at the applicant's application form, we can see that all of the Essential and Desirable criteria seem to have been met, so this candidate Mr. A. Frazer will pass our short-list process. For those who have failed, a sensitive rejection letter needs to be sent out as soon as possible after the closing date for applications.

The Job Application Form

You will almost certainly have your own company application form, either in paper form or on your website.

How accurate is the information given on a job application form? Evidence is that it has become a document that gives people an unrestricted amount of freedom to be creative. Professional organizations exist that will, for a small fee, do the "Killer" application for you. These organizations will provide you with whatever qualification documents you require—all of which will be indistinguishable from the original.

The application form in this book is designed to try and dissuade those undesirable people who are trying to be less than honest. Here are some of the key points worth mentioning:

Photograph

The requirement to provide a current (time bound within the last year) photo of themselves. We need this as a constant reference later in our process.

- Is the person who turns up for testing/profiling the person in the photo?
- Is the person at the interview the person in the photo?
- Finally—is the person who turns up for work the same person?

In 2014, a number of cases were reported where the person who was interviewed was not the person who was tested and interviewed—so let's be ahead of the game on this issue.

Essential Criteria for the Job

By adding these headings into our application form, we restrict the story-tellers, and it also makes short-listing much easier. It helps our applicant to focus and provide us with the best information on which we can assess them.

The Final Page of the Application Form

This rather official-looking page acts as a reminder to the candidate that they will be subjected to testing and that any misleading or untrue information given will result in them being dismissed if they are appointed and this is found out at a later date.

Summary: Step 4

- This step vastly reduces the chance of bias.
- It should be done by someone in HR who is not directly involved in the interview.

- Providing the advert is well written and the Essentials list (criteria) is clear, there is no need to involve the line manager.
- This is the first part of the process where there is a cut on the candidate list. This is your first rejection phase.

Job Application For Finance Manager

An equal-opportunity employer

Thank you for your interest in employment. All applicants will receive consideration for employment without prejudice.

Instructions and Information

To be considered for employment, you must complete this application in full, with complete and correct information. Failure to do so will result in disqualification from consideration for employment and/or termination of employment if you are hired. All application materials submitted will not be returned.

Please type or print legibly. Please complete <u>all</u> areas

Personal Information

Legal Name (Last, First, Middle initial) Frazer, Dai Ali		Email Address Ali@wales.world.com	
Address (Street, City, State, Post Code/Box No.) 15 The Larches, Eastington, West Yorkshire BD1 2PP			
Home Phone 01422 422-22456	Work Phone	May we contact you at work? ☐ Yes ■ No	Mobile Phone 07422 422-22456

Do you have a valid Driving License?	■ Yes/ □ x

For reference purposes, have you worked or attended school under other names? ■ Yes □ No

If yes, list name(s):

Have you previously applied for a position with us?	□ Yes	■ No
If yes, when (month, year)?		
Are you related to anyone currently employed by us?	□ Yes	■ No
List name(s) and relationship:		

How did you find out about this job opening? □ Current Employee   □ Newspaper Ad   ■ Web   □ Other (please specify):

Are you legally authorized to work in this country?	■ Yes	□ No

If appropriate and if employment is offered, you must show documents for verification that prove your identity and employment eligibility.

Attach a current passport-size photograph (no older than 1 year).

EMPLOYMENT HISTORY: List all current and previous employment for the last three positions (including military service), **starting with the most recent position held.**

Dates Employed (month/year) From: Sep 2011 To: Present	Position Title: CFO
Organization Name/Address: ABC Manufacturers Ltd.	

Start Salary £45,000	Final Salary £60,000	■ Full Time □ Part Time

(*Continued*)

May we contact your references? ■ Yes □ No	Manager's Name/Title/Phone: Lord Uppingham 07833 333 227

Reason for Leaving:
Seeking the challenge that this opportunity presents itself.

Duties:
Financial manager, liaising with banks and financiers, overseeing financial reporting for the company, managing the ICT aspects of the finance function, investor relations.

Dates Employed (month/year) From: June 2008 To: Aug 2011	Position Title: Senior Financial Accountant

Organization Name/Address:
Ultimer Fabrics Ltd., Cobbleshaw Lane, Skipton, Yorkshire SK23 6JA

Start Salary £40,000	Final Salary £42,000	■ Full Time □ Part Time

May we contact for references? ■ Yes □ No	Manager's Name/Title/Phone: Apu Patel 0123 543 456782

Reason for Leaving:
Lack of vision of the management.

Duties:
Typical financial duties of an SME including the setting up of the IFRS-based system, cost management, activity-based budgeting.

Dates Employed (month/year) From: May 2003 To: Dec 2007	Position Title: Accounting Assistant

Organization Name/Address:
Adamzale (Mineral Waters) plc, Aitch House, River Street, Canalville, Somerset CV3 4VC

Start Salary £30,000	Final Salary £38,000	■ Full Time □ Part Time

May we contact for references? ■ Yes □ No	Manager's Name/Title/Phone: Peer Gynt 01422 532 8839

Reason for Leaving:
Felt the need to spread my wings.

Duties:
Bookkeeping, trial balance preparation and investigations, ad hoc management accounting exercises, investor relations.

CRIMINAL CONVICTIONS
Have you been convicted of, or plead guilty or no contest to, a crime in the past?
□ Yes ■ No

EDUCATION AND SKILLS—*insert dates as appropriate*

Name of School:	School Location (City):	Qualifications and Grade
Roomfield JM&I	Todmorden, West Yorkshire	Primary school, none
Calderhall Upper School	Todmorden, West Yorkshire	GCSE A–E and 2 A Levels grades B and B

Please list all post-high school education beginning with most recent.

Name, location, and country of University, College, or Institution	Graduated?		PhD/ Diploma	Course of Study
University of Newcastle upon Tyne	■ Yes ☐ No	If no, approximate number of credit hours completed n/a		MBA Degree
No. of years completed: 3 years, part time				
Name, location, and country of University, College, or Institution	Graduated?		PhD/ Diploma	Course of Study
University of Sunderland	■ Yes ☐ No	If no, approximate number of credit hours completed n/a		BA (Business Studies)
No. of years completed: 3 years				
Name, location, and country of University, College, or Institution	Graduated?		PhD/ Diploma	Course of Study
	☐ Yes ☐ No	If no, approximate number of credit hours completed		
No. of years completed				

Note: Applicants for some positions will be required to submit official copies of educational transcripts.

Skills/Certifications:

> List other skills or certifications relevant to this job, including certifications, professional licenses, relevant training, and other relevant knowledge. **Please attach copies of relevant licenses and certifications.**

I am a Qualified Management Accountant (ACMA) and have worked as a finance professional all of my career post university.

One of my strengths is my drive to learn more and more about the company I work with. For example, in a manufacturing company, I will spend as much time as I need in the factory/on the shop floor as I believe it is not possible to be a competent accountant for a manufacturer if you don't understand the products and services they provide.

Moreover, I have become recognized for my long-term, strategic outlook on life: this applies both to my private and my business life. The payoff of this is that I am able to create and maintain credible budgets and forecasts as I am able to turn them into optimal financing and financial management.

In addition to my financial advantages, I have managed teams and worked as part of a team in my various jobs. On more than one occasion, I have won "Manager of the Month" awards, and 2 years ago, I was nominated for CIMA Accountant in the Manufacturing Sector.

I believe I am now ready to take the next step in my career by taking a step up to working with you.

REFERENCES: List three persons who may be contacted as professional references. Do not list family members.

Name (First & Last):	David Tweetie
Address (or PO Box) inc city & Post Code:	15 Cheapside London EC1 3XB
Telephone Number(s):	020 123 654 7890
Email Address:	david.tweetie@ibas.co

Name (First & Last):	Abdul O'Flaherty
Address (or PO Box) inc city & Post Code:	Oscar Wilde House Dublin
Telephone Number(s):	0876 345 1111
Email Address:	AbdulO@gmail.com

Name (First & Last):	Robin P. Thankin
Address (or PO Box) inc city & Post Code:	Batta Tower Wattana Bangkok Thailand 10110
Telephone Number(s):	+66 8544 10477
Email Address:	thakinrp@aistelecomms.co.th

ESSENTIAL CRITERIA FOR THIS POSITION (as referred to in the advertisement)

Clearly explain how you can demonstrate competence in each area—use extra sheets if necessary.

1. Chartered Management Accountant with 15 years' experience in the manufacturing sector, currently operating as CFO of a GBP 75 million turnover company.

   MBA from a highly regarded English University (Cranfield)

2. 15 years' high-quality experience

3. I spent my gap year in France and my sandwich year/internship in head office of a French company. My French language skills allow me to operate without translation and interpretation in a Francophone environment.

4. In my current position, I am the head of a section of around 20 people—7 professionally qualified accountants, 8 accounting technicians, and 5 bookkeepers/trainee accountants.

5. Very early in my career, I was given the responsibility of helping to migrate data from paper to database to financial reports. I have significant experience of working with Sage, Oracle, and SAP. I have significant experience of SAP modules relating to depreciation, payables, and receivables.

6. In 2012, I took and passed the International Financial Accounting Standards Board's Diploma in Financial Reporting. I have been preparing financial statements using IFRS since 2004.

Acknowledgment

I certify that the above statements are true and complete. I understand that any false information or omissions in this application or its supporting documents, or in an interview, will be sufficient grounds for refusal to employ me or, if I am hired, immediate termination without notice. I understand that completion of this application in no way constitutes an offer of employment.

I authorize the company to obtain information about me from my previous employers and credit sources and to review my education, previous employment, driving records, criminal records, references, and other background data. I authorize investigation of all statements contained herein and the references listed above to give you any and all information concerning my previous employment and any pertinent information they may have, and release all parties from all liabilities for any damage that may result from furnishing the same to you.

All employment is subject to testing, profiling, and scored interview prior to selection.

Applicant's Printed Name: Dai Ali Frazer,   Date: February 25, 2015

Applicant's Signature   DOB 1.7. 1979

Approved –
Call for testing

Holding Letter at Short-listing Phase

Letter of acknowledgment—in case you are inundated, Employer's letter in reply to applications for jobs:

> Dear Sir/Madam,
> Re: Post of...
> Thank you for your application dated...
> 201......, in response to our advertisement for the post of.........................

As we have received quite a substantial number of applications, it will take us quite a while to consider each application and short-list the names of the candidates to be called for interview. We envisage that it will take at least 4 weeks.

We shall notify you, either by letter or by telephone, if your name is short-listed.

We thank you for your interest in us and apologize for the inevitable delay in responding to your application.

Yours faithfully,

Human Resources Manager

STEP 5

Testing

Why Do We Do Testing as Part of Our Process?

We know that internationally there is widespread falsification of qualifications. This has been well reported in both the HR press and in international papers. One of the biggest and most widely reported was that of Dr. Obarni. Employed without any testing, he administered a fatal dose of painkiller to one of his first patients who visited him and then fled the country to avoid prosecution. It transpired he has a history of disastrous medical incidents and after a BBC investigation, it was found that it is likely he had never qualified as a medical doctor.

Some of the falsifications of CVs are so good that it would take private detectives months to check them out. Even if a fact on the CV is true, like someone having a degree on a specific topic, there is always the issue of how fresh and up-to-date their knowledge is. We could examine CPE points but have we the time and could we trust them?

What we are trying to establish with testing is, can the candidate do what we want them to do at the level they will be working and in their specialist area within our organization? This applies to all levels in the organization and for all but the most simple of jobs.

About Testing and Its Development

Psychological tests have been shown to be amongst our most powerful aids in the crucial problem of selecting, and developing people at work. Estimates by some researchers have shown, for example, that large increases in the GNP could result from more widespread use of tests in selection. Testing shows us what someone can do today—it will show how the applicants compare not only to each other but also to an external benchmark referred to as a norm group. This can be formed either by occupation or by country data. Tests are now well established and a part of the business selection process. Most of the top performing world-leading companies make use of testing both for selection recruitment and for succession planning.

Tests are now used for all types and levels of job selection: from unskilled factory worker to senior management positions. Most of this usage tends to be in larger organizations, clearly not only because they employ more staff, but also because they have more readily appreciated the difficulties of obtaining top-quality employees.

What Is a Psychometric Test?

An occupational test is simply a psychological test used in the world of work. There have been numerous attempts to define what a psychological test is. One definition for a test is:

"A standardised sample of behaviour which can be described by a numerical scale or category system" (Cronbach, 1984).

Psychological or "psychometric" tests aim to maximize objectivity by standardizing test conditions, instructions, time, content, scoring, and interpretation. All quality tests require that you (the tester) are qualified— this is enforced by both the British Psychological Society and its American counterpart. Quality tests can only be purchased, administered, and interpreted by qualified staff.

Psychometric tools can be divided into two broad categories: knowledge-based and person-based (Rust & Golombok, 1999).

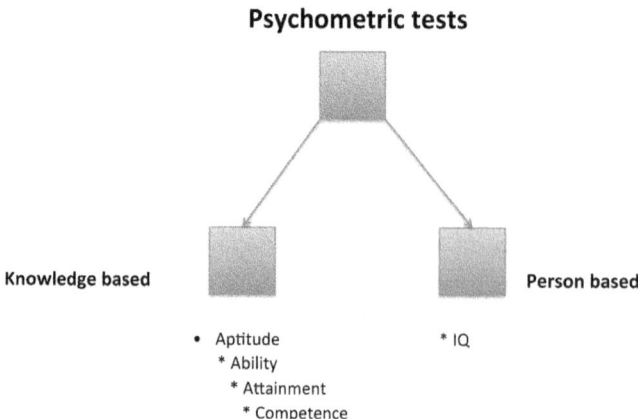

Psychometric tests

Knowledge based

Person based

- Aptitude
  * Ability
    * Attainment
      * Competence

* IQ

1. If we examine knowledge-based first—for our needs in recruitment work application, the tests measure ability, aptitude, attainment, and most importantly competence. These tests conform to the same design principles which are reliability, validity, standardization, and bias avoidance (Anastasi & Urbina, 1997). The tests all have right or wrong answers and the final score is often compared to a norm group. This ensures that you don't select based on the current test group but to the industry norm at the level you are testing for. The "tests" run in strict examination conditions and are always timed. This applies to web-based or pen/pencil face-to-face testing.

2. Person-based; the other form of testing is not widely used in industry and commerce but has a strong following with academics. These include IQ tests and others, which aim to measure general intelligence.

There are all sorts of tests you can use. The skill of the professional interviewer is to use only reliable tests that are valid for the job in hand.

Testing materials are best purchased from reputable suppliers, some of which are as follows:

- British Psychological Society
- Saville and Holdsworth (SHL)
- The Test Agency—Hogrefe
- The Psychological Corporation

Recently, it has been widely accepted by psychologists that ability and personality testing should be measured separately. There is no clear evidence that personality and ability are linked and as a result we have seen testing getting much more focused on work-related ability and knowledge while personality profilers have improved and focus entirely on personality and how this affects one's behaviour in the workplace, despite their skills and abilities.

It is critical for good recruitment that branded tests are used and would advise using only materials from bona fide suppliers. The suppliers will have taken care to check that the validity and reliability trials all complied with the BPS and APS requirements and are fully defendable in case of litigation.

Test Example

Interpreting data—a few questions from a 45-minute battery on data.

This test looks at your ability to understand graphs and statistical tables and to draw appropriate conclusions from them. You will be using facts and figures presented in various ways to answer a range of questions. In each question, you are given five answers to choose from. One and only one of the answers is correct in each case.

Time guideline—not applicable, for illustrative purposes only. Start when you are ready.

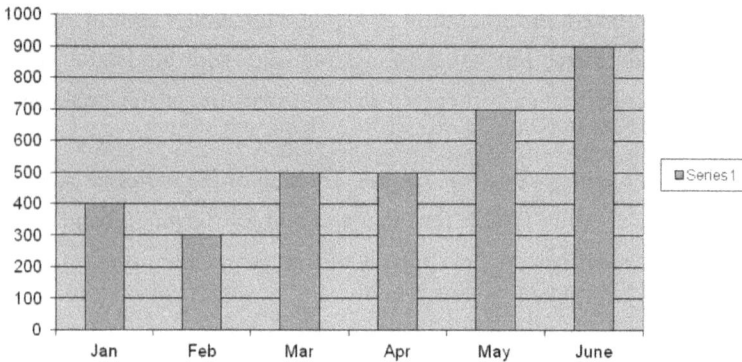

1. How many machines were produced in the first 3 months of this period?

A	B	C	D	E
900	1,000	1,100	1,200	None of these

2. If the trend of the last 3 months continues, how many machines will be produced in July?

A	B	C	D	E
1,100	1,200	1,300	1,400	Cannot say

3. In which month did machine production figures show the greatest percentage change, relative to the previous month?

A	B	C	D	E
February	March	April	May	June

4. What was the combined readership of *Home Hints*, *Travel Plus*, and *Leisure Times* in 2001 (in millions)?

A	B	C	D	E
7.2	16.5	20.8	37.3	None of these

5. What percentage of copies of *Computer News* were sold in specialist computer shops in 2011?

A	B	C	D	E
12%	34%	42%	66%	Cannot say

Magazine title	2001	2011	Subscription	Newsagents
Home Hints	4.8	2.4	47%	13%
Business Tomorrow	1.1	1.4	58%	24%
Computer News	2.3	4.6	34%	24%
Travel Plus	8.5	6.1	25%	44%
Leisure Time	7.5	8	28%	47%

6. If 1.0 million copies of *Travel Plus* were sold by subscription, how many copies were sold overall in 2011 (in millions)?

A	B	C	D	E
1	2.9	4	6.1	8.5

Answers

1. A B C D E
2. A B C D E
3. A B C D E
4. A B C D E
5. A B C D E
6. A B C D E

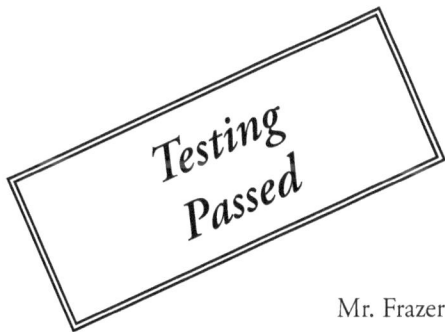

Mr. Frazer

Ability Testing

These are tests which are normally used to test people's ability to do a manual type skill. For example, if you wanted to know if someone could weld dissimilar metals, a simple test could be designed so that they are observed welding dissimilar materials. The test would still need to comply with standard conventions, be valid and reliable, and be administrated by a certified administrator for tests.

An international company that specialized in moving people's belongings had a high incidence of personnel with back injury. No testing had ever been done and the critical requirement for recruitment seemed to be, if you looked big and strong you got the job. A simple lifting test was designed in-house and applicants were scored on whether they lifted correctly according to standard HSE standards and also how careful they were with the object they were moving. This simple test resulted in a massive decrease in reported accidents with newly appointed employees and helped reduce claims from customers for damaged goods.

Semi-medical Tests

Some disorders do not have very obvious symptoms that can be noticed during an interview and therefore are not always picked up by the standard medical form. Specialized testing is needed in order to check whether a candidate has the disorder which could be proved to have very negative effects on their career. Here, we have a few of these disorders which are frequently met in the population and that you should be aware of.

ADHD

What Is It?

Attention deficit hyperactivity disorder (ADHD) or attention deficit disorder (ADD) refers to a range of problematic behaviors associated with poor attention span. These may include impulsiveness, restlessness, and hyperactivity, as well as inattentiveness, and often prevent children from learning and socializing well. ADHD is sometimes referred to as hyperkinetic disorder.

What Are the Symptoms of ADHD?

- Attention difficulties.
- Must have exhibited at least six of the following symptoms for at least 6 months to an extent that is unusual for their age and level of intelligence.
  - Fails to pay close attention to detail or makes careless errors during work or play.
  - Fails to finish tasks or sustain attention in play activities.
  - Seems not to listen to what is said to him or her.
  - Fails to follow through instructions or to finish homework or chores (not because of confrontational behaviour or failure to understand instructions).
  - Disorganized about tasks and activities.
  - Avoids tasks like homework that require sustained mental effort.
  - Loses things necessary for certain tasks or activities, such as pencils, books, or toys.
  - Easily distracted.
  - Forgetful in the course of daily activities.

How Many People Have ADHD?

Consistent and reliable research shows that 3.5% of the population has this disorder. Source: National Clinical Practice and Guidance number 72, commissioned by the National Institute for Health and Clinical Excellence—published by the British Psychological Society and the Royal College of Psychiatrists 2009.

As you can understand, hiring someone with ADHD that is not being treated for it can have very serious consequences not only for them but also for their team at work. They themselves would not be able to keep their focus for long and this would result in not getting things done especially if they were in a position that required micromanaging and working with close attention to detail. On the other hand, a job that did not require the aforementioned qualities would better fit this individual. As far as their team is concerned, a person with ADHD could potentially be described as very distracting by their other team members and this could delay the results of the team.

Color Blindness

What Is It?

There are two types of light-sensitive cells in your eyes called rods and cones. They are both found in the retina which is the layer at the back of your eye that processes images. Rods allow you to see in dim light or at night whereas cones allow you to see in detail and distinguish colors.

There are three types of cone cells: red, green, and blue cones. Each type of cones has a different level of sensitivity to light. When you look at an object, light enters your eyes and stimulates the cone cells. Your brain then interprets the cone cells allowing you to see the color of the object. The red, green, and blue cones all work together to allow you to see the whole spectrum of colors; for example, when the red and green cones are stimulated to a certain level, you will see the color yellow.

Color blindness occurs when one or more types of cones are faulty or missing. This means that you will have difficulty seeing the color that corresponds to the missing or faulty type of cones. For example, if the red cone is missing, you won't be able to see images and objects containing red as clearly.

Most people with color blindness can't distinguish certain shades of red and green.

Types of Color Blindness

Dichromatism

Dichromatism is when one of the types of cones is missing. There are three types of dichromatic color blindness:

- protanopia—the red cones are missing
- deuteranopia—the green cones are missing
- ritanopia—the blue cones are missing

Anomalous Trichromatism

Anomalous trichromatism is when you have all three types of cones but there is a fault in one of them making you less sensitive to certain colors. Again, depending on which cone is faulty, this will cause:

- protanomalous trichromatism—the red cones are less sensitive
- deuteranomalous trichromatism—the green cones are less sensitive
- tritanomalous trichromatism—the blue cones are less sensitive

Red-cone and green-cone defects are known as red-green color blindness.

Monochromatism

Monochromatism is a rare type of color blindness, where none of your cone cells function properly or only one type works as it should. This results in no color vision—all you see is black, white, and shades of gray.

Symptoms of Color Blindness

The main symptom of color blindness is a difficulty in distinguishing colors or making mistakes when identifying them. You may see only a slight difference in different shades of color or if you have severe color blindness, all colors look the same.

In particular situations, this may be made worse; for example:

- in low-level lighting
- if the area of color is small
- if you view a large area of color at a distance
- if you try to distinguish pale colors or dark shades

How Many People Are Color Blind?

8% of men and 0.75% of women —USA and UK major studies

(Source: National Center for Health Statistics USA 2008 and Royal National Institute for the Blind).

Dyslexia

What Is It?

Dyslexia is a neurologically-based, often familial, disorder which interferes with the acquisition and processing of language. Varying in degrees of severity, it is manifested by difficulties in receptive and expressive language, including phonological processing, in reading, writing, spelling, handwriting, and sometimes in arithmetic.

Dyslexia is not the result of lack of motivation, sensory impairment, inadequate instructional or environmental opportunities, or other limiting conditions, but may occur together with these conditions.

Although dyslexia is lifelong, individuals with dyslexia frequently respond successfully to timely and appropriate intervention.

How Many People Suffer from Dyslexia?

It can be as high as 15% of the population in English-speaking societies. (Source: Parliament office of Science and Technology: July 2004 number 226)

Mental Illness

Major Types

Between 8% and 12% of the population experience depression in any 1 year. Schizophrenia is found in 0.06% of the male population and 0.05% of the female population.

(Source 1: The UK office for statistics 2001)
(Source 2: Adult psychiatric Morbidity Survey 2007)

From the above, it is reasonable to conclude that 10% of the population may at any time have mental illness. Therefore, having biodata and even asking for family records can help a recruiter to somewhat predict the possibility of the candidate to develop a disorder that can hinder their professional development.

In conclusion, on the topic of testing—it is unwise to make any appointments without the appropriate testing. This is particularly true as there are so many organizations now offering online qualifications and training organizations who give out certificates just for attendance. With testing, you need to make sure the person who is taking the test is the same person who has applied for the job—always check the photo on the application form with the person you see in front of you.

Summary: Step 5

- You will have many candidates who do not turn up for testing—this is good.
- Always check the photo with the applicant doing the test.
- Testing must be in accordance with the industry guidelines and only be carried out by qualified staff—no exceptions.
- Only use branded materials approved by the BPS or APS.
- This is the second time where you will be failing people in the recruitment process.
- If you are running an assessment center—don't be surprised if some candidates leave because they cannot do it—that's a good thing. Our aim is to have a very strong final interview list.

Reference

Mental Illness
- Source 1: The UK Office for Statistics 2001
- Source 2: Adult Psychiatric Morbidity Survey 2007

ADHD

National Collaborating Centre for Mental Health. (2009). Attention deficit hyperactivity disorder. National Clinical Practice and Guidance number 72, commissioned by the National Institute for Health and Clinical Excellence. Leicester: British Psychological Society and the Royal College of Psychiatrists.

Rust and Golombok 1999

SHL

British Psychological Society

STEP 6

Personality Profiling

Personality profiling is a unique tool for the recruiter. It gives us an opportunity to get a reliable picture of someone's personality and therefore their fit into the job we have on offer. By finding out about the personality, the recruiter can gain insight as to how they will react in a condition of great pressure. Moreover, their interior motives can indicate whether the candidate will be a fit in the organization's general culture.

Why Do We Need This?

It's not rocket science—people whose personality is in line with their job will be happier and should therefore produce better results. Now we have the very instruments to accurately measure personality; and as personality changes very little during one's lifetime and especially adult life (Costa & McCrae, 1997), it's a great predictor of future behaviour in the organization.

It's surprising that more use of personality profilers is not actioned by universities to check that the degree and career someone is following is going to be in line with their personality profile.

Personality profilers give us the opportunity to see if the person applying for the job does in fact have a complementary personality for the type of job they are applying for. This is related to job fit and is not the same as ability.

Progress of Personality Profiles

The top profilers today are accurate and of immense use for recruiting, promotion selection, and development. However, there is a big caution here: there are thousands of profiles that are available—most are not personality profilers but Type indicators. Type indicators are designed to put you neatly into a pigeon hole—you're one of these or one of those. They do not fit our requirements for interviewing and many would not pass close examination if they were challenged for relevance. Their attraction is that they are quick to do, cheap and in the main, that they can be used by not highly specialized personnel.

What Profilers Should We Use?

For recruitment of someone up to a supervisory level, the most frequently recommended are the NEO or the EPI. Both are about 60 questions and, in particular, the NEO is very fast to score.

For more senior personnel recruitment, development of succession planning is the most appropriate choice. Some of the best tools for it on the market are as follows:

- NEO-PIR
- SHL OPQ32 (expensive)
- MPA (very new)
- Cattell 16PF (rather old)
- Holden HPI—sometimes difficult if feedback is needed
- Hogan scales (HPI, HDS, MVPI)

All of the profiles listed, and this is not an exhaustive list, require the user to be qualified, either through the supplier or via the British or American Psychological societies.

Profile 1: The Eysenck EPI

Eysenck suggests that there are three fundamental (higher-order) unrelated (orthogonal) traits: extraversion, neuroticism and psychoticism (Eysenck, Eysenck, & Barrett, 1985). These traits, which can be measured and described on a continuum, are biologically based and have many behavioral implications. Two traits – extraversion and neuroticism—have, however, been most investigated at the biological, information-processing and motivational level. Thus findings on extraversion suggest it is substantially biologically inherited. It is explained in terms of cortical arousal and reward sensitivity and it has been suggested that extroverts succeed in high-pressure jobs that involve considerable interaction with strangers. They handle overload and stress, have task-focused coping, feelings of self-efficacy and a good sense of well-being. Neuroticism, also based on biological factors to a great extent and high in heritability, is associated with stress vulnerability, sensitivity to punishment and threat avoidance. Neurotics portray highly selective biases in cognitive processes with considerable awareness of danger, cautious decision-making, a generally negative self-concept and often depressed mood and pessimistic outlooks.

Introverts and Extroverts

A review of the dimension presents an impressive array of findings. Introverts are more sensitive to pain than are extroverts; they become fatigued and bored more easily than do extroverts; excitement interferes with their performance, whereas it enhances the performance of extroverts and they tend to be more careful but slower than extroverts.

The following are some additional differences that have been found:

Introverts do better in school than extroverts, particularly in more advanced subjects. Also, students withdrawing from college for academic reasons tend to be extroverts whereas those who withdraw for psychiatric reasons tend to be introverts.

Extroverts prefer vocations involving interactions with other people whereas introverts tend to prefer more solitary areas of expertise. Extroverts seek diversion from job routine; introverts have less need for novelty. Extroverts enjoy explicit sexual and aggressive humor, whereas introverts prefer more intellectual forms of humor, such as puns and subtle jokes.

Extroverts are more active sexually, in terms of frequency and different partners, than introverts are. Extroverts are more suggestible than introverts. Introverts are more easily aroused by events and more easily learn social prohibitions than extroverts. As a result, introverts are more restrained and inhibited. There is also some evidence that introverts are more influenced by punishments in learning, whereas extroverts are more influenced by rewards. It is hypothesized that individual differences along this dimension have both hereditary and environmental origins. Indeed, several studies of identical and fraternal twins suggest that heredity plays a major part in accounting for differences between individuals in their scores on this dimension.

Extroverts are more likely than introverts to prefer occupations that involve social contact. There is, therefore, a danger that introverted workers may become over-aroused if their jobs involve considerable extra organizational contact and a relative absence of routine. Blunt (1978) argued that introverted managers would thus tend to choose positions involving relatively routine duties (finance, production, or technical managers), whereas extroverted managers would be more likely to select jobs in sales, marketing, or transport. The results were broadly as hypothesized, except that transport managers were less extroverted and production managers more extroverted than predicted.

Successful businessmen are on the whole stable introverts; they are stable regardless of what type of work they do within business, but then a degree of extroversion may be related to type of work. The data are probably reasonably reliable because relatively few respondents failed to answer, and because scores on the scale did not indicate any market tendency to "fake good".

The results suggest that the EPI may have some modest role to play in furthering research into the personality patterns of persons engaged in business and industry. The notion that introverted workers are better able to handle routine work activities than extraverted ones was investigated by Cooper & Payne (1967) in a study carried out in the packing department of a tobacco factory where the work was repetitive and light. Job adjustment, as assessed by two supervisors, was negatively related to extraversion and those workers who left the job in the 12 months after testing were significantly more extraverted than those who remained. Neuroticism was also implicated, being related to poor job adjustment and to frequency of non-permitted absence. The use of both conditioning and arousal theory is evident in the thinking of Cooper & Payne (1967):

Because extroverts condition poorly and introverts readily, extroverts are less able to tolerate tasks of a routine nature, since inhibition accumulates and inhibits sustained task performance.

Because extroverts are under-aroused, they seek arousal and do not function as well as introverts with a minimal or moderate sensory variation input. Various studies have found extroverts to be bored by monotonous tasks and hence do them poorly.

It would seem that the extroverted subjects do not merely prefer to be in the company of others, but that their work efficiency actually improves in the face of distractions, while the solitary preference of the introverts is reflected in their reduced efficiency of work when distracted. Paying heed to such preferences, as measured by the Eysenck Personality Inventory, is therefore not only a method of increasing contentment at work by means of personnel selection, but should also result in improved efficiency of output.

Profile 2: Cattell's 16PF

Perhaps the most famous of all personality tests applied to industrial, organizational, and occupational settings is Cattell's (1971a) 16PF, first published over 40 years ago. For Cattell, the test has several advantages: it is unusually comprehensive in its coverage of personality dimensions; it is based on the functional measurement of previously located natural personality structures; the measurements are relatable to an organized and integrated body of practice and theoretical knowledge in clinical education and industrial psychology.

The test measures 16 dimensions of personality (and six to nine second-order factors) which are supposedly independent and identifiable, and reliably and validly measurable. The psychometric properties of the scale are well documented, as is the problem of deception (people faking on it). The test has been around so long, is very shrewdly and aggressively marketed in a variety of countries, and Cattell himself has been such an active researcher and zealous advocate of the test, that it has attracted incredible attention. For instance, if one consulted the handbook printed 25 years ago (Cattell, Eber, & Tatsuoka, 1970), one would find incredible evidence of the application of the test. These data are in fact divided into two sections. The first concerns available specification equations against criteria: various weights are given (per personality dimension), derived from multiple regressions, to specific measurable job-success criteria. Policemen to school counselors are considered.

For example, consider the following, where the letters (A, B, C, etc.) refer to one or other of the 16 traits and the numbers (.44, −.11, etc.) to the weighting of each:

Salesmen: Retail. Two studies, the larger by Industrial Psychology Inc., have related actual sales volume in comparable situations (retail bakery route salesmen, soft-drink salesmen) with the following average equation:

$$\text{Salesmanship} = .44A - .11B + .11C - .22E + .11F - .11G + .22H - .33L - .11M + .11N + .11O + .44Q + .22Q3 - .22Q4 + 1.87 \text{ [Group mean} = 5.56].$$

In this case, even the smaller weights have been retained because the sign was the same in the two studies. It will be clear from this, as from some other instances, that the popular stereotypes and impressions on which occupational selections are still often based can be erroneous. Thus, dominance, E+, is actually not effective in face-to-face selling, and the view of the successful salesman as an "extrovert" has to be modified. For although gains are shown through exviant deviations (the temperament source traits of A, F, and H), self-sufficiency, Qa, is actually oppositely weighted to the extrovert direction; i.e., the inviant endowment is required.

Salesmen: Wholesale. On wholesale (gram) salesmen, personality has similarly been correlated with actual sales income, resulting in the following equation:

$$\text{Wholesale Sales Success} = .21A + .10B + .10C + .10E + .21F + .10G - .10L - .31M + .21N - 31Q + .21Q3 - 21Q4 + 3.80 \text{ [Group mean} = 5.09].$$

It should be noted that intelligence shifts to a positive effect here, autism (M) is more of a drawback than it was in the retail field, and so on, but otherwise there is a "family similarity" between the two types of sales activity. (Cattell et al., 1970)

Secondly, equations are derived and cross-validated on samples. Occupations as varied as accountants to athletes, military cadets to musicians, and sales personnel to social workers, are considered. For example, in the case of executives and industrial supervisors, Cattell et al. (1970: 199) noted:

Perhaps the classing together of several types of executives has smoothed out some special characteristics that will later be found; but at present, except for high warmth, intelligence, and independence, the profile diverges little from that of "the man in the street". However, the characteristics are in the direction that psychological analysis would suggest, namely, a high tolerance of people in affectothymia (A+), toughness in Factor H, shrewdness in N, some self-development in (Q3+), and a marked willingness to try new ideas and new methods (Ql). At the second order, the executives are not high in criteria (QIII) as one might expect, and the chief characteristics are some independence and exvia. The pattern for the supermarket personnel is one of interpersonal warmth (A+), as might be expected, but it is clearly not a sales pattern, nor even an exviant (extroverted) one. A glance at the second-order anxiety component (CD, OQ, Q4+, L+) shows an appreciably raised anxiety level, and one wonders about the degree to which the personal tensions and detailed cares of the manager's position have produced this, or the degree to which a position of this kind simply tolerates performance by quite anxious persons. The sober desurgency (FD) seems consistent with individual difference variables selected for examination. Although there is general consensus about the dependent variable that is considered (i.e., job satisfaction; minor psychiatric morbidity; blood pressure), there seems to be theoretical consensus as to what type of individual difference variable to consider. However, one variable that has been examined extensively and to the relative neglect of nearly all others has been the "Type A" behavior pattern.

Profile 3: Costa and McCrae's "Big Five" NEO and NEO–PIR

The direct inheritor of the Eysenckian and Cattelltian traditions are the Americans Costa and McCrae, whose work in the 1980s and 1990s revived the world of personality theory and testing. Working within the psychometric trait tradition, they settled on three and then five dimensions of personality. Now called the "five-factor approach" (FFA) or "five-factor model" (FFM), there is now broad agreement on the approach/model, including those who adopt the lexical approach—that is, those who look at natural language and the relationship between everyday terms for personality traits (Goldberg, 1992). Indeed, there is an active psycho-lexical tradition in personality the theory which attempts to "recover" the basic dimensions of personality through analysis of natural language. Researchers have found impressive evidence, across various different languages, of the emergence of similar factors which are analogous to the "Big Five". What they have not done, however, is to look at the association between personality traits and work outcomes. There are vigorous critiques of the FFM, but these have not reduced its popularity among personality researchers (Block, 1995; Eysenck, 1992).

Costa and McCrae (1985) argue that there are five basic unrelated dimensions of personality. These are Extroversion, Neuroticism, Agreeableness, Conscientiousness, and Openness to experience. According to the researchers, each individual's personality can be described as combinations of the aforementioned traits. Each of the "Big Five" is a spectrum of the characteristic and everyone has some degree in each of them. For example, someone high in extroversion can be characterized as an extrovert and someone very low in it, as an introvert. All individuals have different personalities because these are made of unique combinations of the traits.

A second body of research has been to compare the NEO-PI as the questionnaire is called, with other measures. A third, perhaps most important topic of applied research has been to examine the validity of the measure—that is, to examine what the test scores predict. The test has been applied to various sorts of worlds.

However, it is in the world of work that organizational behavior researchers have become most interested in the FFM. It has proved a robust and reliable measure. For instance, Piedmont and Weinstein (1994) related the NEO-PI factor scores with four supervisor ratings: adaptive capacity, task orientation, interpersonal relations, and overall rating. They found that, whereas the correlations between conscientiousness and all four ratings were significantly positive and between extroversion it was so with three out of the four (not the overall rating), neither Openness to experience nor Agreeableness was related to any of the ratings.

Yet, what is clear from this literature is that, whereas some personality dimensions are good predictors of job proficiency, not all are. This is for at least three reasons. First, quite logically, different traits relate to different behaviours and, if a trait is unrelated to a particular occupational behaviour, it is unlikely that the two are correlated. Thus, high neuroticism seems related only to "negative" behaviour at work, such as absenteeism, but not to such things as productivity. This was the point made so clearly by Robertson and Kinder (1993). They showed that if there were good theoretical reasons to suppose certain specific traits (from a large battery) were related to specific measurable work outcome variables, the validity coefficients were around .20 but could rise to .30.

Integration of Personality Measures with the FFM

This method was used in various reviews of criterion validity (Barrick & Mount, 1991; Tett et al., 1991). For example, Barrick and Mount (1991) conducted a large-scale meta-analysis of 117 validity studies and a total sample that ranged from 14,236 people for Openness to Experience to 19,721 for Conscientiousness. Performance measures within these groups were classified into three broad criteria: job proficiency, training proficiency, and personnel data. Barrick and Mount (1991) reported that Conscientiousness was consistently found to be a valid predictor for five occupational groups and for performance criteria. However, the other four personality factors only generalize their validity for some occupations and some criteria. Extraversion was observed to be a valid predictor (across the criterion types) for two occupations, managers and sales people. Emotional Stability was a valid predictor for police officers; Agreeableness was a valid predictor for police officers and managers; while Openness to Experience was found to predict the training proficiency criterion relatively well, as did Emotional Stability and Agreeableness. Similarly, Openness to Experience was not found to be a valid predictor of job proficiency or personnel data. In a follow-up study, Mount and Barrick (1995) found that overall validity of Conscientiousness has been underestimated and that the overall score and both of its dimensions (dependability and achievement) predicted specific performance criteria better than global criteria (e.g., overall rating of job performance). Tett et al. (1991) used only confirmatory studies—that is, studies based on hypothesis testing or on personality-orientated job analysis. Mean validities derived from confirmatory studies were considerably higher than those derived from exploratory studies. These results generally supported those reported by Barrick and Mount (1991), but are distinctly more positive for the predictive validity of traits. In essence, Tett et al. (1991) found that all personality dimensions were valid predictors of job performance.

Profile 4: Saville & Holdsworth's Occupational Personality Questionnaire

Sometimes, commercial organizations, rather than academic researchers, devise personality measures to be sold as diagnostic instruments. One such organization, which has expanded greatly over the past 20 years all around the world, is Saville & Holdsworth Ltd. (SHL, 1984), which claims several advantages for its Occupational Personality Questionnaire (OPQ). It is said to be based on a conceptual model providing compre-hensive coverage of personality and to be psychometrically sound. It is also designed to be easily used in occupational contexts.

The most comprehensive version of the OPQ measure consists of 30 items derived from a conceptual model based on existing personality inventories, repertory grid studies and criteria for occupational success, with an additional social desirability scale. The items are grouped into three categories associated with relationships with people, thinking style, and feelings and emotions, respectively. The OPQ manual presents data showing that the 30 "concept model" items have generally satisfactory internal consistency and test–retest reliability.

Although the amount of empirical research on the OPQ is much less than that on the EPQ, the 16PF, or the NEO-PI mentioned earlier, it is growing. The advantage it has over the other questionnaires is not so much its theoretical basis or psychometric properties, but the database of thousands and thousands of working people around the world who have completed it. This means it is by far the most expensive profiler with users paying a license fee each year—this does not include any materials (Furnham, Race, & Rosen, 2014).

Profile 5: Hogan Personality Measurements (HPI, HDS, MVPI)

Hogan and Hogan (2001) developed these three scales to measure different aspects of personality, accompanied by a fourth measure called MATRIGMA, which measures intelligence. The first scale, namely the HPI, measures the bright side of an individual's personality and consists of seven characteristics. The higher one scores in these, the more they guide their behavior in the workplace. On the other hand, the HDS measures the dark side of personality. As various researchers have shown (e.g., Dotlich & Cairo, 2003; Oldham & Morris, 1995), there are 11 personality traits that correspond to specific personality disorders that can lead to the derailment of a leader. More specifically, these traits, match the personality disorders in a subclinical level, and manifest when an employee or even a CEO is under a lot of pressure or when all their guards are down.

The aforementioned scales help the recruiters to identify whether a candidate will do well in the position for which they have applied. The MVPI, on the other hand, offers a more specific view on the person's fit to the organization. The MVPI measures the extent to which an individual is motivated by specific values. In other words, what the candidate will need from the culture of the company in order to be fully satisfied from working there. This is not only helpful for the recruiter, but also for the potential employee, since they will be able to figure whether they will be content in the specific working environment, after doing some research on the organization's culture to see if it matches their motivators. It has to be noted, that low scores on some of the 10 motives does not necessarily mean that this factor acts as a demotivator but that rather, the individual is indifferent to that.

The only disadvantages of this measure are that it is particularly expensive and it can only be used by certified individuals.

For more senior posts, there are only a few to choose from; NEO PI-R, or OPQ by SHL are firm favorites.

In the NEO–PIR example shown here, we have a candidate (Mr. Frazer) who has applied for our Finance vacancy, passed the short-listing, and also passed the testing with very high scores. The profiling shows, however, that the candidate's fit for the job is far from our requirements. This true example illustrates how ability and personality can be very

NEO PI-R™ Personality Inventory UK Edition

Profile Sheet

Personal Details:	Name	Date of Birth	Date	ID number
	D. A FRAZER	1·7·1979	25th Feb 2015	

Equal Opportunities Monitoring:	Gender	male	Ethnic Origin	White Euro	Norm Group used	m

Facet Scores

			Raw	T	T	Very low 20 25 30 35	Low 40 45	Average 50 55	High 60 65	Very high 70 75 80
N	1	Anxiety							● 60	
	2	Angry Hostility					● 40			
	3	Depression				● 25				
	4	Self-Consciousness				● 20				
	5	Impulsiveness								● 80
	6	Vulnerability				● 30				
E	1	Warmth				● 25				
	2	Gregariousness								● 70
	3	Assertiveness								● 70
	4	Activity								● 80
	5	Excitement Seeking								● 80
	6	Positive Emotion								● 80
O	1	Fantasy								● 70
	2	Aesthetics				● 35				
	3	Feelings				● 25				
	4	Actions							● 60	
	5	Ideas							● 60	
	6	Values				● 25				
A	1	Trust				● 25				
	2	Straightforwardness				● 25				
	3	Altruism				● 25				
	4	Compliance				● 25				
	5	Modesty				● 20				
	6	Tender Mindedness				● 20				
C	1	Competence							● 60	
	2	Order								
	3	Dutifulness				● 35				
	4	Achievement Striving								● 80
	5	Self Discipline								● 80
	6	Deliberation								● 80

Unsuitable — Do not call for interview

HOGREFE
THE TEST PEOPLE

different. Take a few moments and see for yourself how unsuited this person would be.

Assessment Centers: What Are They?

"Assessment Center" is a term used to describe any event where the skills and abilities of individuals are assessed using a variety of techniques. Most commonly, assessment centers consist of "exercises" that are designed to give a measure of the key skills needed to carry out the job effectively. The best assessment center exercises aim to mimic the job as far as is possible.

Although assessment centers have been around for some time, their popularity followed the assessing of Officer Potential in the Armed Forces during the last war. All of the Services use assessment centers today. The uptake of assessment centers in a commercial setting was advanced in the United States and has been a feature of the selection and assessment practices of many organizations—the trend is one of increased growth due to its validity and proven results.

During an Assessment Center, individuals will take part in a variety of different activities.

- These may include:
  - group work
  - one-to-one interviews/role plays
  - written work
  - testing
  - personality profiling
- The exercises are designed to draw out relevant standards of performance for the target level of management or job family. The event is designed to assess individuals against the predetermined success factor levels.
- The exercises are also designed to simulate as closely as possible the type of activity found in the target role or level. If it is not possible to simulate the on-the-job tasks, then different activities will be substituted which will enable the same behaviors to be assessed.

- The exercises will be observed and assessed by trained in-company observers, guided by experienced assessors. The results are immediately scored as they take place.
- During the event, the candidates will be chaperoned by the assessor. He/she will explain the exercises and activities and offer support and guidance as needed.
- At the end of the event, the observations and assessments of performance are pooled in a "wash up" discussion. At this stage, the observers will agree on the level of performance and potential and whether to accept the candidates or not.

One of the great strengths that assessment centers have is the ability to measure and observe candidates over a significant amount of time. Many companies do assessment centers over a two-day period and include a formal dinner so that candidates can be seen in a nontested environment.

Assessment centers mainly show how well the candidate can function in a team. In the actual job, they will be part of a specific team so gaining insight to their attitudes as team players is really useful. Moreover, getting to meet the candidates in a nonwork environment such as a dinner as mentioned above, shows how well they can fit with the other team members, which extends to their organizational fit.

References

Costa, P., & McCrae, R. (1997). Longitudinal stability of adult personality. In Hogan, R., Johnson, J., & Briggs, S. (Eds.), Handbook of Personality Psychology (269–290). San Diego: Academic Press.

Dotlich, D., & Cairo, P. (2003). Why CEOs Fail. San Francisco: Jossey-Bass.

Eysenck, S., Eysenck, H., & Barrett, P. (1985). A revised version of the psychoticism scale. Personality and Individual Differences, 6(1), 21–29.

Furnham, A., Race, M.-C., & Rosen, A. (2014). Emotional intelligence and the Occupational Personality Questionnaire (OPQ). Frontiers in Psychology, 5, 1–8.

Hogan, R., & Hogan, J. (2001). Assessing leadership: A view from the dark side. International Journal of Selection and Assessment, 9, 40–51.

Oldham, J., & Morris, L. (1995). New Personality Self-Portrait: Why You Think, Work, Love and Act the Way You Do. New York: Bantam Books.

STEP 7

Finalizing the Interview Questions

There is really not much to do here, but it does give you the time to check through each of the criteria and make sure that all the knowledge-based questions make sense. It's at this stage that the questions are written onto the marking sheets and it must be clear who is asking the questions for each set of criteria. It is preferable if the professional interviewer starts off the questioning and the line manager asks all the probing questions. Questions need to be scored at the end of each question; so it's 10 points for a perfect answer regardless of how many probing questions are asked (maximum of 4 per question). Do not be tempted to add in obvious questions such as the ones shown below. Stick specifically to questions from your Essentials list.

Questions to Avoid

Tell me about yourself

Where do you see yourself in the next five years?

What are your strengths and what are your weaknesses?

What do you know about our company?

Let me ask you some questions about your CV

The only materials you should need for the interview are the Interview question sheets for each candidate and, of course, the all-important photograph; the CV became redundant immediately after the short-listing.

Interview standard questions

JOB .... Candidate ....

Date .... Interviewer ....

Scene setter	Score
1	
2	
3	
4	
Score	

STEP 8

Pre-Interview Administration

Every time you interview someone, it's really a high-level PR exercise. You want to attract, engage, and employ good candidates. Very often in large organizations, the interview preparation is poor to say the least; extra effort should be made to get it right the first time, which means involving all parties in the interview chain.

Letter/email for appointment. Clear instructions on where you are, where to park, and exact time of the interview. Those involved in the first welcoming are security and the receptionist. They should also be informed about who will be coming in, their purpose of visit which in this case is the interview, and what time this will happen. Forgetting to inform these people can result in misunderstandings and frustration to both sides; the candidate can become really stressed due to this and consequently underperform in the interview, as also the organization's image can be negatively affected as miscommunication is perceived as a significant flaw.

Setting up of the room. The interview room needs to work for you; forget all the nonsense about round table or no tables, just use what you have but where the candidate sits is very important. (see diagram)

Why is this position so important—it gives you the best possible opportunity to observe their **body language**, in particular, you are looking to see if they are telling truths when answering probing questions.

So What Do We Look For?

Understanding and being able to decode body language is a very important and useful skill to have. Men always want to know how to tell if women like them and women always want to know how to tell when men are lying. Although these are interesting thing to know, finding out more about body language is a complex and involved subject. Here are some areas that will help.

Baton Signals

Baton signals are ways that we can enforce serious messages by using principally our hand and arms. Baton signals are great for conference work, when training others, or when making a convincing sales pitch.

The palms up and shown: this is a classical "trust me" pose, if the arms are then extended exposing the chest it communicates "trust me—I have nothing to hide."

The same using the right hand and arm, known as the one hand intention touch is another very convincing gesture, used with a sweeping motion and accompanied with the words "I'm sure you will agree." This move is great to use when you have to quickly convince a group of people and for use by trainers.

If you are giving a talk or if you are running a training session—the next baton signal is of great use to you. This is the stop sign. If you have someone in a group who interrupts you, this is a powerful way of getting control. Please be careful as this has to be used correctly and with the correct supporting words.

Let's assume you are giving a presentation to a group of people and you have said "I will take all questions at the end." You are in the middle of your tale and someone interrupts, you could say, "please I will take questions at the end." This may or may not work. It would be far more powerful if you reinforced this by first a palm vertical signal, rather like a stop sign, then immediately as you speak with the same hand a sweep to the right—follow on by adding "let's move on."

Agreement Signals

Sitting forward, leaning forward, and slight head nodding are all good body signals to show you're in agreement. Interviewers need to be careful here as people often "fake" this, particularly those who have done some reading on body language. Other agreement signals particularly when seated at a desk are "hand steeples". Hands together as if praying with fingertips pointed slightly forward normally accompanied by the words "I'm in complete agreement with you."

Disagreement Signals

These are easy to spot if you are alert. Slight shaking of the head, looking away, if seated, moving back in the seat, arms crossed: these are all signals to watch for.

I Like You, Signals

Men

Men show liking by smiling more and by frequent touching of their hair or tie—this is very evident when they are talking to a woman they like. Men will also stand nearer to people they like and always face them.

Women

Women often display larger pupils in their eyes when they really like someone (male or female); this is very easy to see in blue-eyed people and if it's a man will play with or touch, flick their hair frequently. If they are wearing a scarf, then they will make numerous adjustments to it.

Telling Lies

Detecting when people tell lies is very important. The 99.9% method to do this is to use a brain scanner and you will observe a certain area of the brain heating up when the person lies. Although this is interesting, we can't pop someone into a scanner every time we think they are not telling the truth. Frequent nose touching and in general face touching is usually interpreted as showing that the person is lying. When telling a lie, people will feel uncomfortable and thus will engage in small and unneeded moves. Touching the face adds to that because it is perceived as helping someone hide, which can be justified when one is lying.

As this is very important for negotiators and HR people, interviewing professionals and the police, we will look at the wide spectrum of what we can see through observing body language.

The Simple Signs

When people tell lies, the simple signs are:
- Hand over the mouth or close to the mouth
- Breaking off eye contact
- Shifting around (squirming)
- Men get sensitive in the neck area and will sometimes touch or rub their necks
- Women sometimes get red in the front of the neck

More Complex Signals

Most people believe that liars give themselves away by what they do, rather than what they say or how they say it. The best indicators of complex lying are to be found in people's speech and in their body language.

CIRCUMLOCUTION: Liars often beat about the bush. They tend to give long-winded explanations with lots of digressions, but when they're asked a question they're likely to give a short answer.

OUTLINING: Liars' explanations are painted with broad brushstrokes, with very little attention to detail. There's seldom any mention of time, place, or people's feelings. For example, a liar will tell you that he went for a pizza, but he probably won't tell you where he went or what kind of pizza he ordered. When liars do provide details, they are seldom in a position to elaborate on them. So, if you ask a liar to expand on his account, it's very likely that he'll simply repeat himself. When a truth-teller is asked the same question, he usually offers lots of new information.

SMOKESCREENS: Liars often produce answers that are designed to confuse—they sound as if they make sense, but they don't. Examples of remarks that don't make sense include Bill Clinton's famous response during the Paula Jones harassment case, when he was asked about his relationship with Monica Lewinsky, and answered, "That depends on what the meaning of 'is' is." Another example is the justification that the ex-mayor of New York City, David Dinkins, gave when he was accused of failing to pay his taxes: "I haven't committed a crime. What I did was fail to comply with the law."

NEGATIVES: Political lies are frequently couched in the form of a denial—remember Bill Clinton's famous denial, "I did not have sexual relations with that woman, Miss Lewinsky." When a politician denies that he is going to introduce a new measure, like raising taxes, you can usually take this as a sign that the measure is about to be introduced. As Otto von Bismarck said, "Never believe anything in politics until it has been officially denied." Liars are more likely to use negative statements. For example, during the Watergate scandal, President Nixon said "I am not a crook." He didn't say "I am an honest man."

WORD CHOICE: Liars make fewer references to themselves—they use words like "I," "me," and "mine" less frequently than people who are telling the truth. Liars also tend to generalize by making frequent use of words like "always," "never," "nobody," and "everyone," thereby mentally distancing themselves from the lie.

DISCLAIMERS: Liars are more likely to use disclaimers such as "You won't believe this", "I know this sounds strange, but. . . ," and "Let me assure you." Disclaimers like these are designed to acknowledge any suspicion the other person may feel in order to discount it.

FORMALITY: When people are telling the truth in an informal situation, they are more likely to use an elided form—for example, to say "don't" instead of "do not." Someone who is telling a lie in the same situation is more likely to say "do not" instead of "don't." That's because people become more tense and formal when they lie.

TENSE: Without realizing it, liars have a tendency to increase the psychological distance between themselves and the event they're describing. As we have seen, one way they do this is by their choice of words. Another is by using the past tense rather than the present tense.

SPEED: Telling a lie requires a lot of mental work because, in addition to constructing a credible line, the liar needs to keep the truth separated from the lie. This places demands on the capacities of the liar, which in turn can slow him down. That's why people pause before producing a lie, and why lies tend to be delivered at a slower pace than the truth—unless, of course, the lie has been carefully rehearsed, in which case there should be no difference in speed.

PAUSES: Liars also produce more pauses between their words and sentences, and some of these pauses are filled with speech disfluencies like "urn" and "er."

PITCH: The pitch of someone's voice is often a very good indicator of their emotional state, because when people get upset the pitch of their voice starts to rise. Emotions are closely connected to vocal pitch and the changes that occur when people become emotional are very difficult to mask or conceal. Although increases in pitch are fairly consistent, they are sometimes quite small, and it is usually necessary to have heard someone speaking in other situations before one can decide whether the pitch of their voice has risen.

To conclude, to spot a lie, you should always focus on a broad range of behavioral and speech clues. If you think you can spot a liar on the basis of a single clue, you're deceiving yourself. Work involved in producing a spontaneous lie also gives rise to more speech errors, slips of the tongue, and false starts, where the person starts a sentence and then abandons it for another sentence.

The purpose of watching body language is to see if further probing questions are needed. You must be careful and not turn the interview into an interrogation. Moreover, you have to be very careful about which signs of body language you interpret and in what way, because all this research on body language has made us prone to over-interpreting and sometimes exaggerating about the meaning of a movement.

Positioning of a Clock

Don't make the mistake of removing your watch from your wrist or having your mobile phone on the desk. It simply conveys that you are more interested in the time than the candidate. A clock should be sited behind the candidate and with easy sight of you, the professional interviewer.

Drinks

Water on the table is fine—keep it refreshed and make sure there is a good supply of clean drinking glasses. Avoid giving the candidate tea or coffee as both are diuretics.

Make Sure

The room is tidy—it's part of the PR exercise. No mobile phones, not on silent or vibrate but off. Ensure that there is clear sign posting and the room has a "Do not disturb—interviews in progress" displayed on the door.

Summary: Step 8

- Preparation is the key to success.
- It is the professional interviewer's responsibility to get everything right—not the line manager's.
- Small details do matter—brief those who need to know and if you're a lists person—have a checklist.

- The only documentation you need for the interview is the Interview questions sheets and the candidate's photograph. The CV has no further use.
- The use of interpreting body language is your responsibility to check and is an indicator to ask further probing questions— don't overdo it.

Reference

Morris, D. (2006). People watching: The Desmond Morris Guide to Body Language. London: Vintage Books. http://www.amazon.co.uk/Peoplewatching-Desmond-Morris-Guide-Language/dp/0099429780/ref=sr_1_fkmr1_2?s=books&ie=UTF8&qid=1424939493&sr=1-2-fkmr1&keywords=manwatching+Dr+Desmond+Morris.

Brown, W. Rtd FBI Polygraph examiner How to spot liars.

Pease, A., & Pease, B. (2006). The Definitive Book of Body Language. New York: Bantam Books.

STEP 9

The Interview

Most of the work has been done—all that's left is to run the interview in a very professional way and stick exactly to the pre-written questions on your question sheets for each of the criteria.

Timing

The timing for the interview should be perfect—if not, it's your fault and shows the organization in a bad light.

How many interviews in a day?

Six is about right, three in the morning and three in the afternoon. It's all about quality, not quantity.

Dress Code

Be smart, you represent the company you need to look the part—make sure that the interviewing line manager is aware. Your aim is to be as sharp, professional, and smart at the end of the day as you were for the first interview.

Who Does What?

The interviewer should be responsible for collecting the candidate and seeing them to and from the room in a relaxed but professional manner.

The interviewer should then set the scene for how the interview is to run—this needs to be learnt by rote to avoid fumbling or bumbling at the start of the interview—a good crisp introduction that we use is as follows:

"Please let me explain how this interview will run—we will ask you a series of questions about your experience, please give short and concise answers. At the end of the interview, you will have the opportunity to ask us any questions you may have—is that OK?"

The interviewer should then start—our first series of questions is about team work (scene setter). Reading from the question paper, you ask the first question.

If the answer is perfect, then you would score 10 on your sheet. Always write the score immediately after the question and do so in a light blue pen (you don't want the candidate to be too aware of the scoring).

If the answer requires clarification, then you can ask probing questions. The score will still be out of 10.

Tricks Some Candidates Might Use

C: Could you repeat the question?
I: The question would be read back exactly the same.
C: I don't understand the question—can you explain it.

WARNING: If you do this, you will be giving this candidate an advantage over the others.
I: Let me repeat it again.

If the candidate still does not understand, simply and smoothly move on to the next question—the score would then be 0.

When interviewing with nontrained managers, they seem to think it's their duty to help the candidate as much as they can. However, this can potentially cause chaos as it is highly possible that it gives rise to a significant amount of biases. Candidates who have been trained in interviewing skills will take maximum advantage of this.

Interviewing fresh college or university leavers requires a completely different approach and this is shown in Appendix 1.

A run-through of some questions, answers, and scoring follows:

For each series of questions, the pre-question sheet is completed with the appropriate knowledge-based questions written on it. This would be done at the time the advertisement is discussed.

Scene setter Working with Teams	Score
1 What experience have you had at managing teams in the past 5 years?	
2 Give me an example where you have dealt with conflict in a team	
3 From your experience, what is the optimum size for an effective team?	
4 Do you encourage competition between teams?	
Total Score	

Interviewer

Good Morning—this is Mr. Said—he is head of Finance and will be interviewing with me.

We will be asking you a number of questions about your past experience. Please give short and concise answers to the questions. When we have finished the questions at the end of the interview, you will have the opportunity to ask us any questions that you have—is that OK?

Scene setter—"we will now ask you a series of questions on working with teams"

Q. 1: *Interviewer*

> What experience have you had at managing teams in the past 5 years?

A. Interviewee: I have run a department of 50 people for the last 5 years.

Interviewer probing question? • *Were they split into teams?*

A. Interviewee: Yes by function, when I first took on the job it was just one department, but dividing the department into teams worked really well.

Interviewer probing question? • *Whose idea was it?*

A. Interviewee: Mine.

Interviewer probing question? • *What were the benefits?*

A. Interviewee: We were better equipped to meet or deadlines, never missed any so far, and unauthorized absence stopped. Also, there is a much better working environment.

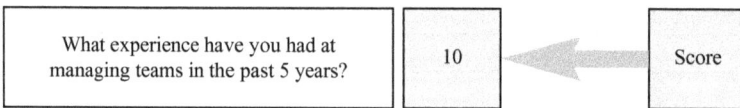

What experience have you had at managing teams in the past 5 years?	10	⬅ Score

The Second Question on Team Working

Q. 2: *Interviewer*

> Give me an example where you have dealt with conflict in a team.

A. Interviewee: We had one employee who was very disruptive—always talking on his mobile phone and texting.

Interviewer probing question? • *How were you involved?*

A. Interviewee: Some of the team complained about him to me, I then spoke to him on a one to one and pointed out this was not acceptable in our department.

Interviewer probing question? • *Did that resolve the issue?*

A. Interviewee: No, he took no notice so I had to give him a verbal warning in accordance with our procedures—that brought an immediate stop to the problem, he was not happy but understood why I had to pursue the matter.

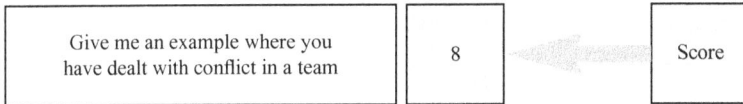

Give me an example where you have dealt with conflict in a team	8	Score

Q.3: *Interviewer*

From your experience, what is the optimum size for an effective team?

A. Interviewee: I don't understand the question.

Q. Interviewer: *From your experience, what is the optimum size for an effective team?*

A. Interviewee: Sorry, I don't understand would you rephrase the question?

Q. Interviewer: *Don't worry—let's move onto the next question.*

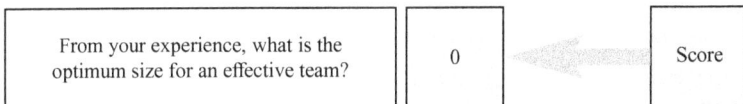

From your experience, what is the optimum size for an effective team?	0	Score

Q. 4 *Interviewer*

Do you encourage competition between teams?

A. Interviewee: Yes, it's a good thing providing it's well-controlled. This is particularly the case when we do end of year accounts and we have a special payment system for the best teams. We get good results and the teams all like a bit of competition. Last year, the winning team brought cakes for all the rest, which was really appreciated; also the end-of-year accounts were completed 2 days ahead of schedule, so the CFO was very happy.

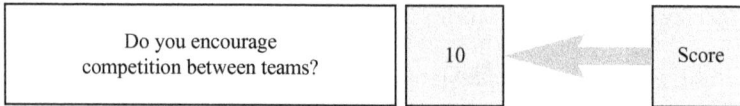

Do you encourage competition between teams?	10	Score

Interviewer:

Scene setter—the next series of questions are about current accounting processes

When each interview is finished, check that all the scoring has been completed—this is not a time to make up scores after the event. You should be able to tell the candidate when they will have the outcome of their interview. If you promise a date, make sure you keep to it, and don't be vague with statements like "hopefully sometime next week."

At the end of your interviewing day(s), the candidate who has the highest score gets the job. If you have all six candidates with exactly the same scores, then the tie-break is in the test results and the person with the highest test results gets the job.

Some Issues to Keep in Mind

There has been a lot of research regarding the validity and reliability of interviews. The two major aspects of these are the following two questions: whether interviewers agree with each other and also, whether the answers that candidates give during interviews do indeed predict future performance (Chamorro-Premuzic & Furnham, 2010). In order to increase the reliability, interviewers need to be trained not only on what questions to ask and why to ask them, but also on how to interpret them. In this way, personal biases will be eliminated to a great degree. Moreover, as far as increasing the validity of interviews is concerned, it is crucial that interviewers make their decisions only based on salient facts and are very careful as to notice and ignore any impression-management techniques that the candidate might use.

The Post-Interview Procedure

The post-interview procedure is very important. The interviewer should ring up the successful candidate—be very upbeat—they have worked hard and spent a lot of time and effort to get a job with you.

Likewise, when you contact the unsuccessful candidates, ring up and speak to them. They deserve a BIG thank you for all their hard work; and remember, you have a key PR role here.

Although not strictly part of the interview, what is often poorly managed are the first few days of the successful candidate's post. A VIP welcome should be the standard for every new person and this needs careful planning and executing. It has been shown that our initial reactions are the ones that stick, so it's in everyone's interest to do a good job. This point is very well made in the book "It's our Ship" by Captain D Michael Abrashoff—the first chapter says it all.

Skype Interviews, Social Media, and References

Skype interviews are a very efficient way of interviewing particularly if the candidate is in another country. The same process applies and the same steps need to be in place. It is extremely important that you watch the person carefully during the interview (check with the photo you have that it's the right person)—long pauses and looking away by the candidate could suggest someone else is feeding them the answers. A recent case of Manik Sharma highlighted this problem as the candidate was referring to a book for the answers. He was employed and later fired for being incompetent and unqualified—a very expensive mistake.

Finding out more about the candidate is just common sense—have a look at Facebook and Twitter and see what they are doing out of work.

The actual written reference is very unhelpful. Employers are reluctant to give any detailed information in case they are accused of spoiling someone's job chances. An informal telephone call with their current employer will probably be more effective.

In the Ubarni case, it was found that both of the references furnished were given by people who hardly knew him at all. He was employed based on a very fabricated CV and references alone. On his first assignment as an out-of-hours GP, he administered a fatal drug overdose to a patient who later died. So much for his glowing references—it was later mooted that Dr. Ubarni was unqualified.

All of this reinforces the real need for testing as in stage five of our process, ignore it at your peril.

Probation Periods

See Appendix 3

Reference

Chamorro-Premuzic, T., & Furnham, A. (2010). The Psychology of Personnel Selection. Cambridge: Cambridge University Press.

APPENDIX 1

Some questions for Fresh Graduates/College leavers

Management Qualities—Criteria Sign Posts

Area	Competency Definition
Leadership	Motivates and empowers others in order to reach organizational goals.
Planning & Organizing	Organizes and schedules events, activities, and resources. Sets up and monitors timescales and plans.
Quality Orientation	Shows awareness of goals and standards. Follows through to ensure that quality and productivity standards are met.
Persuasiveness	Influences, convinces, or impresses others in a way that results in acceptance, agreement, or behavior change.

Sign Post—Questions on Leadership

Score out of 10

1. Describe an example of a time when you had to coordinate the work of other people.
   - What were you trying to achieve?
   - How did you go about organizing the work?
   - What feedback did you have about your style of coordinating tasks? ☐
2. Tell me about a time when your input motivated others to reach a team goal.
   - Why was this necessary?
   - What did you do to motivate the team?
   - Why did this work? ☐

3. Give me an example of a time when you successfully helped someone to carry out a task independently.
   - How did you enable them to carry out the work?
   - How did you follow this up?
   - What was the outcome? □
4. Tell me about a situation when you found it difficult to focus the work of a team on an objective.
   - What made this work difficult?
   - How did you try to overcome these difficulties?
   - How could you improve upon this? □
5. What opportunities have you had to identify development opportunities for others?
   - What action did you take?
   - Why was this important?
   - What impact did this have? □
6. We all have times when we find it difficult to control the activities of others. Give me an example of when you faced this type of situation.
   - Why did you find the situation challenging?
   - How did you overcome the difficulties you faced? □

Sign Post—Questions on Planning and Organizing

1. Tell me about how you normally cope with a lot of work.
   - Where do you start?
   - What do you do to ensure it all gets done?
   - What prevents you from getting it all done? □
2. Give me an example of when you had to organize a piece of work, project, or an event.
   - How did you prepare and plan for it?
   - What time scales did you set?
   - How well did it go? □
3. Give me an example of when you had to work to an important deadline.
   - How manageable were your timescales?
   - What did you do to ensure that the deadline was met?
   - What did you learn? □

4. Describe the last time you missed a deadline.
   - Why did this happen?
   - How responsible were you for this?
   - What did you do to try to overcome the problem? ☐
5. Describe a time when you had to organize the implementation of a plan.
   - On what basis did you determine your priorities?
   - How did this work out in practice? ☐
6. Even the most organized individuals may find that they overlook some of the activities required in planning an initiative. Tell me about a time when this happened to you.
   - What were the consequences of this?
   - How did you try to rectify this?
   - What was the outcome? ☐

Sign Post—Questions on Quality Orientation

1. Give me an example of when you have had to produce high-quality work.
   - Why did the work have to be of such a high standard?
   - How did you ensure that these standards were met?
   - What feedback did you get regarding the quality of this work? ☐
2. What sort of professional standards have you had to adhere to in the past?
   - Why were they important?
   - What difficulties did you encounter maintaining them?
   - How did you ensure that others also complied with these standards? ☐
3. Describe a time when you did not meet your usual standards of work.
   - What alerted you to this?
   - How did you overcome the problem?
   - What were the long-term consequences? ☐

4. Tell me about a time when you have had to achieve a work goal in a limited time.
   - How important was it?
   - What did you do to ensure that you achieved the target?
   - What feedback did you have about the quality of this work?   ☐

5. Give me an example of a time when you had to check that productivity standards were met.
   - Why was this work important?
   - How did you monitor progress?
   - What did you find?   ☐

6. Sometimes, getting a task finished on time means that the quality of work/service is compromised. Give me an example of when this happened to you.
   - What issues or implications did you anticipate?
   - With whom did you consult?   ☐

7. Working to a high standard can be difficult, especially when we must rely on the work of others to achieve our goals. When have you had to do this?
   - What methods do you employ to encourage a sense of standards in others?
   - Give me an example of when you put this into practice.
   - What was the response of the other people?   ☐

Sign Post Questions on Persuasiveness

1. Tell me about the last time you won someone over to your point of view.
   - How did your opinion contrast with their original position?
   - What were the key things that you did which persuaded them?
   - What kind of agreement did you reach?   ☐

2. Give me a recent example of when you negotiated a successful outcome.
   - What did you negotiate?
   - How did you win the person around?
   - How did you know that they were really convinced?   ☐

3. What are your strengths in terms of influencing people?
   - How often do you find yourself influencing others?
   - How do you compare to others in this area?
   - What could you do to make yourself more effective at influencing others?

4. Give me an example of a time when you were unable to persuade someone around to your point of view.
   - Why was this important?
   - Why did you not succeed?
   - What have you learnt?

5. There are times when no one is prepared to listen or agree with your point of view. Give me an example of when this happened to you.
   - How did you present your point of view/idea?
   - What were the objections?
   - How hard did you push your viewpoint?
   - Where did you leave the conversation?

6. For most of us, the occasion arises when we must convince others to make an unpopular choice/decision. Give me an example of when you had to push an unpopular choice/decision.
   - How did you try to get others on board?
   - What was the result?
   - With hindsight, how could you have approached this differently?

7. Some people are easier to persuade than others. Which people do you find it hard to persuade?
   - What is it that makes persuading them so difficult?

TOTAL SCORE Maximum 260

APPENDIX 2

Interview Standard Questions

JOB .... Candidate ....

Date .... Interviewer ....

Scene setter	Score
1	
2	
3	
4	
Score	

APPENDIX 3

Probation

It is always wise, wherever and whenever possible, to place newly recruited employees on probation. Probationary periods can vary from 3 months to a year. In fact, for many public sector appointments, the probationary period can be as long as 3 years.

Human resource managers should explain to every new employee that the term *probation* in the context of employment means precisely "a trial working period" before the position of the employee is confirmed or terminated. Probationary periods serve both employees and employers well.

During such periods, either party will have the opportunity to decide accordingly. The employee will be able to decide whether or not to continue with the job, while the employer will be able to decide whether or not the employee can cope with the duties and responsibilities entrusted to him/her.

Usually, during the probationary period, new employees are given opportunities to learn as much as they can about their jobs. The onus is on the department concerned to ensure that ample opportunities are given to these new employees to learn as much as they possibly can learn from their assigned jobs. Department managers should keep records of the progress made by the new employees during the probationary period. These records will enable them to advise the human resource personnel department as to whether or not the employees can be confirmed in their jobs at the end of their probation. If it is felt that a new employee requires more time and given such extra time will make the grade, then the period of probation can be further extended. The employee should be tactfully told this, lest he/she may feel slighted or hurt at not being confirmed and may eventually decide to leave.

It will be in the best interests of all concerned if the human resource department can organize a counseling session to explain the reason for the extended period of probation.

Nonetheless, it is the duty of the employer to notify the employee at the end of the probation whether or not he/she is to be confirmed. (In most cases, such a letter would still come from the human resource department, anyway.)

The employer should also notify the employee of the decision to either extend probation or to terminate his/her services before the expiry of the probationary period.

Failure to do so can bring about several confusing conclusions.

The employer may consequently assume that the employee is confirmed in his/her employment. The employee, likewise, can assume that as his/her job is secure, he/she is therefore considered confirmed in his/her position.

Therefore, to avoid any unnecessary adverse interpretation of the situation, it is in the best interests of the company to notify the employee in writing of its decision.

Under normal practice, the employee is informed in writing by his/her department manager whether he/she is to be confirmed in his/her job.

Usually, a letter confirming such appointment also carries some form of congratulatory message for his/her having successfully met all the requirements of the department during the probationary period.

The letter, which very often comes from the human resource department, also contains some form of a welcoming message.

It is also important that the employee be informed if there is any salary adjustment, now that he/she is confirmed.

Similarly, it is important to advise any new employee in writing if he/she cannot be confirmed. It is also quite in order to state categorically the reasons for him/her not being confirmed in the post.

It is also in order to state in such letters whether the employee's probationary period is to be extended further to enable him or her to improve. Otherwise, a simple letter terminating the services will suffice.

In such a termination letter, it is appropriate to state the reason for the termination.

The human resource department should advise the employees under probation of their status at the end of their probationary periods.

The human resource department manager may perhaps wish to prepare better ones with more personal or formal content.

Some human resource department managers who are constantly involved with these tasks normally keep stacks of such standard letters for various occasions, including notifying employees of their status at the end of their probation. This is quite a common practice among labor-intensive corporations.

It is wise to advise the employee concerned in order to avoid complications.

Credits

Research

Principal Researcher
Luke Treglown
Research Assistant, UCL
Psychology Undergraduate, University of Bath
&
Kelly Petropoulou
Research Assistant,
University College London

Illustrations

Noel Ford

Examples

- Personality Profile Hogrefe—the test people for use of the NEO-PIR
- Short version of a test—Mark Parkinson—Psychometric Test
- SHL

Graphic Design and Printing

Graphic Impressions—Chelmsford—www.graphic-impressions.co.uk

Photography

Mathew Ph2o Photography Limited—Chelmsford

Proofreading

Stan Keller, www.proofchecker.com

Index

OTHER TITLES IN THE HUMAN RESOURCE MANAGEMENT AND ORGANIZATIONAL BEHAVIOR COLLECTION

Announcing the Business Expert Press Digital Library

Concise e-books business students need for classroom and research

This book can also be purchased in an e-book collection by your library as

- *a one-time purchase,*
- *that is owned forever,*
- *allows for simultaneous readers,*
- *has no restrictions on printing, and*
- *can be downloaded as PDFs from within the library community.*

Our digital library collections are a great solution to beat the rising cost of textbooks. E-books can be loaded into their course management systems or onto students' e-book readers. The Business **Expert Press digital** libraries are very affordable, with no obligation to buy in future years. For more information, please visit **www.businessexpertpress.com/librarians**. To set up a trial in the United States, please email **sales@businessexpertpress.com**.